BILLY GRAHAM

150
ESSENTIAL
INSIGHTS ON
FAITH

HARVEST HOUSE PUBLISHERS
EUGENE, OREGON

Cover design by Bryce Williamson

Cover photo © venimo / Gettyimages

Interior design by Chad Dougherty

Content development by Meadow's Edge Group LLC. Thank you, Seamus Dillon at Zondervan and Marshall Shelley at Christianity Today, for helping make this book possible. Your kindness and graciousness are exemplary.

For bulk, special sales, or ministry purchases, please call 1 (800) 547-8979.
Email: Customerservice@hhpbooks.com

M is a federally registered trademark of The Hawkins Children's LLC. Harvest House Publishers, Inc., is the exclusive licensee of the trademark.

150 Essential Insights on Faith

ISBN 978-0-7369-8220-7 (pbk.)
ISBN 978-0-7369-8221-4 (eBook)

Printed in the United States of America

21 22 23 24 25 26 27 28 / VP-CD / 10 9 8 7 6 5 4 3 2 1

This book includes material from these sources:

Todd Hafer, private interviews with Billy Graham (August and September, 1992).

Harold Myra and Marshall Shelley, The Leadership Secrets of Billy Graham (Zondervan, 2005). Used by permission.

Ralph Keyes, The Quote Verifier (St. Martin's Press, 2006).

Todd Hafer, editor, For Your Confirmation: Promises and Prayers (Hallmark, 2009). Used by permission.

Billy Graham, Just as I Am: The Autobiography of Billy Graham (Zondervan, 1997). Used by permission.

Ruth Graham, A Legacy of Faith: Things I Learned from My Father (Zondervan, 2006). Used by permission.

Press conferences and public addresses.

CONTENTS

*Go into all the world and preach the
gospel to the whole creation.*

MARK 16:15

INTRODUCTION

Billy Graham. A spiritual confidant to US presidents beginning with Harry Truman. A respected adviser to myriad world figures, from Winston Churchill to Boris Yeltsin to Ronald Reagan to Bono. For more than seven decades, Mr. Graham spoke to hundreds of millions of people in more than 185 countries and territories—from massive crusades in major cities to small gatherings in remote African villages. He appeared more than fifty times on the Gallup organization's "Ten Most Admired Men in the World" poll. He also received the Congressional Gold Medal and was honored by the George Washington Carver Memorial Institute for his contribution to race relations.

Well into his nineties, Billy Graham continued to proclaim his message of hope, encouragement, and faith through televised crusades, a worldwide radio ministry, an internationally syndicated newspaper column, and appearances on programs like *Larry King Live*.

Mr. Graham wrote more than thirty books, including several *New York Times* bestsellers.

Raised on a North Carolina dairy farm during the Great Depression, Billy Graham maintained a humble spirit and singular goal throughout his long ministry. "My purpose in life," he said, "is to help people find a personal relationship with God."

This book features highlights from Mr. Graham's life and ministry. You'll discover stirring quotes, fascinating anecdotes, and profound spiritual insights sure to capture the mind and the heart.

We hope and pray that this book will give you new insights into a remarkable man—and that his wise words will inspire and encourage you and draw you closer to the God whom Billy Graham served so faithfully.

THE HEART OF THE BILLY GRAHAM MESSAGE

I am eager to preach the good news.

ROMANS 1:15

I recall an old Methodist preacher who came to Harringay Arena in London in 1954. "I have come here every night for ninety-three nights," he told us, "and I have heard only one message." He meant it as a compliment, for he knew as I did that there is **ONLY ONE** Christian message.

God created us in His image.
He created us and **LOVES** us so
that we may live in harmony and
fellowship **WITH HIM**. We are not
here by chance. God **PUT US HERE**
for a **PURPOSE**, and our lives are
never fulfilled and complete until His
purpose becomes the **FOUNDATION**
and center of our lives.

God provided **HIS LOVE** on the cross. When Christ hung, bled, and died, it was God saying to the world, **"I LOVE YOU."**

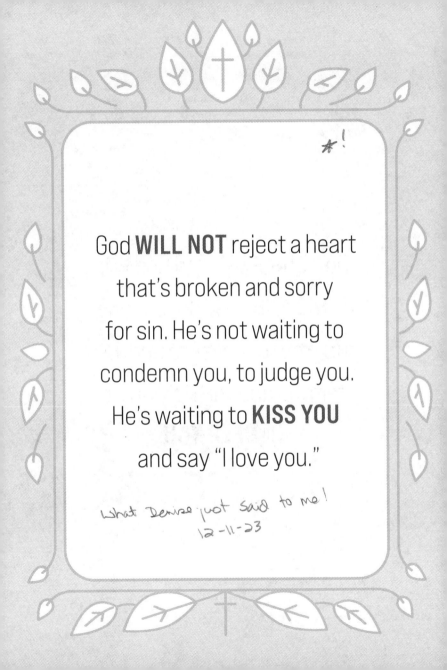

God **WILL NOT** reject a heart
that's broken and sorry
for sin. He's not waiting to
condemn you, to judge you.
He's waiting to **KISS YOU**
and say "I love you."

What Denise just said to me!
12-11-23

Do **YOUR PART** and God will do **HIS PART**. Work hard and turn the rest over to God. Be faithful and the Holy Spirit will **HELP YOU**.

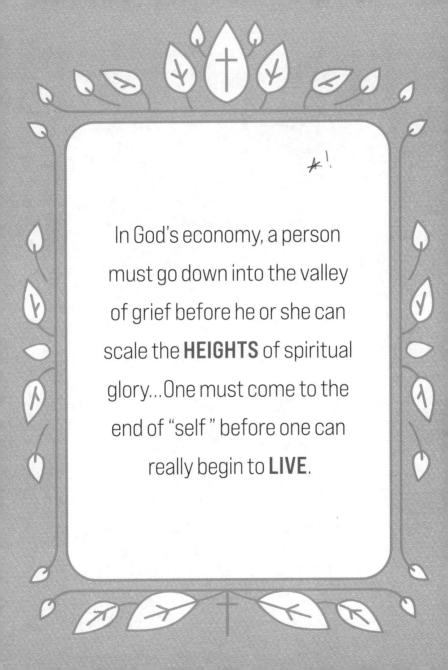

In God's economy, a person must go down into the valley of grief before he or she can scale the **HEIGHTS** of spiritual glory…One must come to the end of "self" before one can really begin to **LIVE**.

Unless the soul is **FED** and **EXERCISED** daily, it becomes weak and shriveled. It remains discontented, confused, restless.

Tears shed for self are tears of weakness, but tears shed **FOR OTHERS** are a sign of **STRENGTH**.

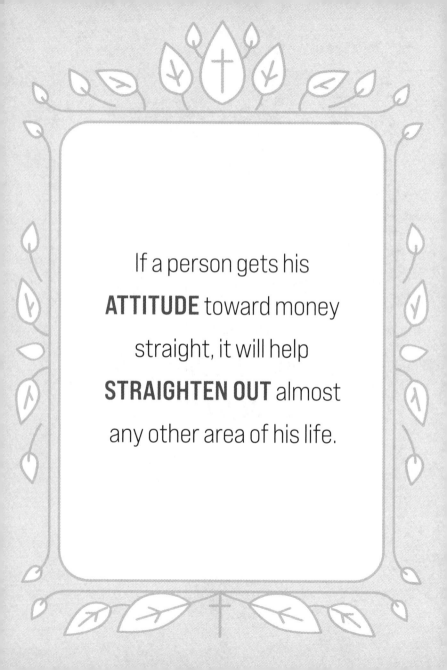

If a person gets his **ATTITUDE** toward money straight, it will help **STRAIGHTEN OUT** almost any other area of his life.

One of the greatest tenets
of the Christian faith is **LOVE**,
and "love" is an **ACTIVE WORD**.
We are to go **OUT OF OUR WAY**
to love people who perhaps
we don't like or who have
a different skin color or a
different ethnic background.

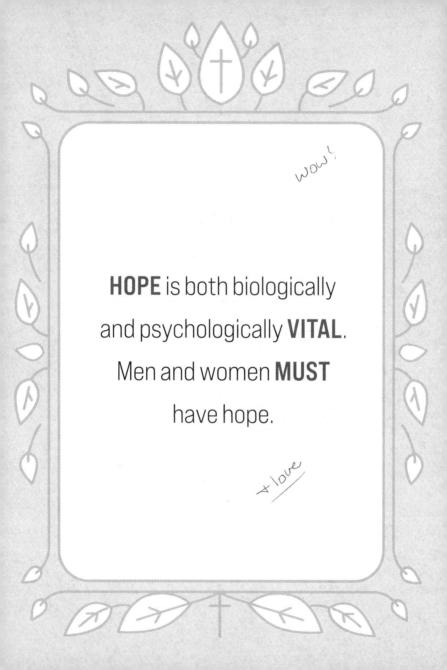

wow!

HOPE is both biologically
and psychologically **VITAL**.
Men and women **MUST**
have hope.

+ love

[Speaking after the 1995 Oklahoma City bombing]

Times like this will do one of two things: They will either make us hard and bitter and angry at God, or they will make us **TENDER** and **OPEN** and help us to reach out in **TRUST** and **FAITH**. I pray that you will not let bitterness and poison creep into your souls, but that you will **TURN IN FAITH** and **TRUST** in **GOD**, even if we cannot understand.

ON FRIENDS AND FAMILY

Show family affection to one another with brotherly love.

ROMANS 12:10

In my ministry, I've been blessed by the people who have surrounded me and worked with me. Without men like Cliff Barrows, Bev Shea, T.W. Wilson, Bill Brown, Guy Martin, Allan Emery, and George Bennett—and all the other people who have served on our board and worked on the crusades—our ministry would be nothing. You would have never heard of me. I give all the credit and glory on this earth to them. And **ALL THE GLORY** we give collectively to **GOD**, because without His Holy Spirit, we couldn't have done it.

Everybody needs some friends around him who will say, "You are wrong!" And that includes me. I really value the **FRIENDSHIP** of people who'll just tell it to me **LIKE IT IS**, even though I may try to defend my position for a while.

Ruth and I are

HAPPILY

incompatible.

Given our own family situation, I have only respect and sympathy for the courageous and committed single parents who for a while (or a lifetime) have to carry the burden alone. The secret of Ruth's survival was in her **COMMITMENT**—not only ~to God~ her marriage commitment before God or her love for me, but also her ministry commitment of the two of us to the **LORD'S PURPOSE** for our lives together.

I want to say to Ruth, my **DEEPEST LOVE** for a companion who has been with me ever since 1943 as my **WIFE**: I love her with all my heart.

UNITY IN DIVERSITY

Above all, put on love—the perfect bond of unity.

COLOSSIANS 3:14

Jesus said, "Go ye into **ALL THE WORLD** and preach the gospel." He didn't say, "Go into the capitalist countries only." I've been in countries with right-wing dictatorships. I've been in countries that have left-wing dictatorships. But I've tried **TO STAY RIGHT** with the **GOSPEL OF CHRIST** and stay out of the various political situations.

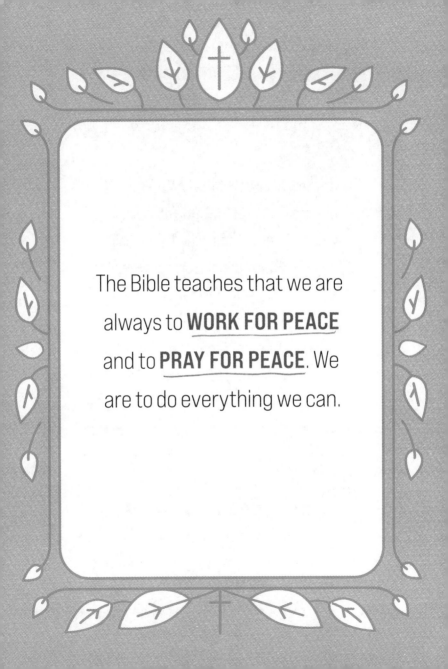

The Bible teaches that we are always to **WORK FOR PEACE** and to **PRAY FOR PEACE**. We are to do everything we can.

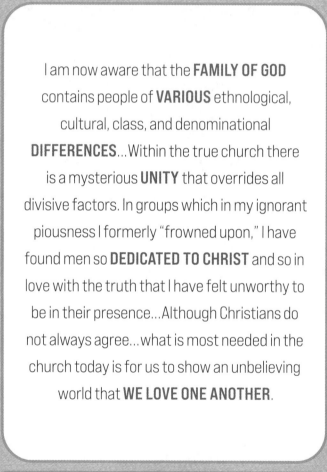

I am now aware that the **FAMILY OF GOD** contains people of **VARIOUS** ethnological, cultural, class, and denominational **DIFFERENCES**…Within the true church there is a mysterious **UNITY** that overrides all divisive factors. In groups which in my ignorant piousness I formerly "frowned upon," I have found men so **DEDICATED TO CHRIST** and so in love with the truth that I have felt unworthy to be in their presence…Although Christians do not always agree…what is most needed in the church today is for us to show an unbelieving world that **WE LOVE ONE ANOTHER**.

We have to stand in the **MIDDLE** in order to preach to all people, right and left. I haven't been faithful to my own advice in the past. I will be in the future. I'm not for the left wing or the right wing. I'm for the **WHOLE BIRD**.

I don't believe that we should cut ourselves off from people with whom we disagree. I think we ought to talk to them, try to understand their point of view, and let them understand our point of view. I don't think the church ought to have this terrible division in which we don't even speak to each other. I went to the World Council of Churches in New Delhi, and I went to the National Association of Evangelicals in Denver. I go to all these different groups because I believe that the church is **BIGGER** than any one little group. God has His people in **MANY PLACES**, and I think we are going to be surprised when we get to heaven to find out who is there and who is not there.

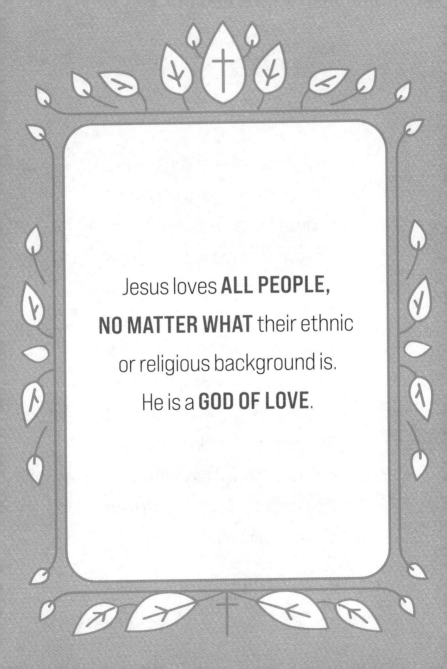

Jesus loves **ALL PEOPLE,**
NO MATTER WHAT their ethnic
or religious background is.
He is a **GOD OF LOVE**.

I think a spirit of hostility is wrong. I believe that we should **LOVE**. Regarding those who criticize me from all points, I have asked God a thousand times, "Lord, give me love for them." I don't believe I can preach with liberty unless **GOD HAS GIVEN** me this love and this **MATTER IS CRUCIFIED** in me, until I can say with all my heart that I do love them and could sit down and talk with them, eat with them, fellowship with them, and pray with them—anything!

Satan would like nothing better than to have us stop our ministry and start answering critics, tracking down wretched lies and malicious stories. By **GOD'S GRACE** I shall continue to preach the **GOSPEL** of Jesus Christ and not stoop to mudslinging, name-calling, and petty little fights over nonessentials.

I think the church is going to have to **RENEW** itself for a **NEW DAY** and take a **NEW APPROACH** to hold people who made commitments to Christ under various circumstances.

I'm for **MORALITY**, but morality goes beyond sex to **HUMAN FREEDOM** and **SOCIAL JUSTICE**. Evangelists cannot be closely identified with any particular party. We have to stand in the **MIDDLE** in order to preach to all people.

I have really never been a
fighter at heart and do not like
to engage in sharp answers.
I believe that a **SOFT ANSWER**
turns away wrath.

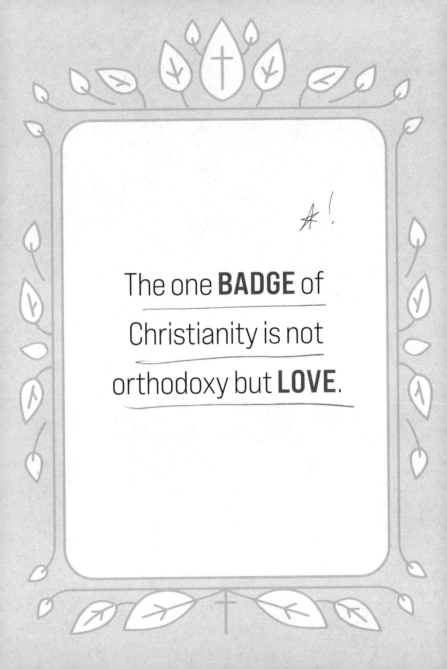

The one **BADGE** of
Christianity is not
orthodoxy but **LOVE**.

A MAN AND HIS MISSION

Good news from a distant land
is like cold water to a parched throat.

PROVERBS 25:25

All of our work and frail human attempts are nothing without **GOD'S BLESSING**, brought about by **PRAYER** and **TRUST IN HIM**. As we look at the years ahead, I pray that God will **STRENGTHEN US** and that we will **NOT LOSE HEART**. For He "is able to do immeasurably **MORE** than all we **ASK** or **IMAGINE**, according to his **POWER** that is at work within us" (Ephesians 3:20 NIV).

The **TEST** of a preacher is that his congregation goes away saying not, "What a lovely sermon!" but "I will **DO SOMETHING**."

(On conversions at Billy Graham crusades)

In some cases they are not lasting at all. In other cases they are **ABSOLUTELY PERMANENT**. In every single country of Africa and South America that we have visited, I have met people who got their start in an encounter with Christ at one of these crusades and are now **SERVING HIM** as missionaries or social workers or medical people...

...We believe that this is the work of God, and that in each city we come to, there are people whose **HEARTS** are already **PREPARED** by the Spirit of God. They make a **PROFESSION OF FAITH** and it lasts because **GOD DOES IT**. This happened to me.

I believe in the **SOVEREIGNTY** of God. God chooses His **SERVANTS**. I believe that God chose me for this particular task at this moment, but whether it is more successful than the work of others whom you have never heard of, I doubt. I think the most **SUCCESSFUL** people are probably individuals whom we will never hear about until we get to **HEAVEN**.

When I first heard myself called an **EVANGELIST**, I resented it. I thought of Elmer Gantry. But I've come to like it. It comes from a Greek word meaning "proclaimer;" an evangelist is a **PROCLAIMER** of the **GOOD NEWS** that God **LOVES** us and wants to **HELP** us.

Like it or not, money is an essential part of any ministry, and safeguards must be put in place to avoid abuses or misunderstandings and to handle all finances with **INTEGRITY** and **OPENNESS**…

…Most of our financial support comes from the thousands of people who send contributions to us every month. We have **NO LARGE FOUNDATIONS** behind us, and we are dependent on relatively small gifts to meet our expenses every year.

I want to give God all the **GLORY** and all the **PRAISE** for what has been accomplished in my life and those of my family and associates. I look forward to the day when I can see Jesus **FACE TO FACE** and lay at His feet any honor I've ever received, because **HE DESERVES IT ALL**.

I don't put myself up as a prophet or someone whom a nation needs. I would say all the nations need the **PREACHING OF THE GOSPEL**. I am an evangelist. The word "evangelist" comes from the Greek word *keryx,* which means "proclaimer." I am a **PROCLAIMER** of the message of the Bible. I am not preaching some new idea, some new philosophy, or something I have thought up. I am simply **PREACHING THE BIBLE**, the same old truths that the church has believed for centuries.

Being a **CHRISTIAN** is more than just an instantaneous conversion—it is a **DAILY PROCESS** whereby you grow to become **MORE LIKE CHRIST**.

When we come to a large city, all the controversies within the church are brought into focus by the crusade. The tension is not in us; it is already there. There are those who, for one reason or another, feel they cannot support the meetings. I never answer them, I never mention them, I never attack them. I **RESPECT** their point of view, but we go on **PREACHING THE GOSPEL**.

The tendency among some evangelists was to exaggerate their successes or to claim higher attendance numbers than they really had.

We **COMMITTED** ourselves to **INTEGRITY** in our publicity and our reporting.

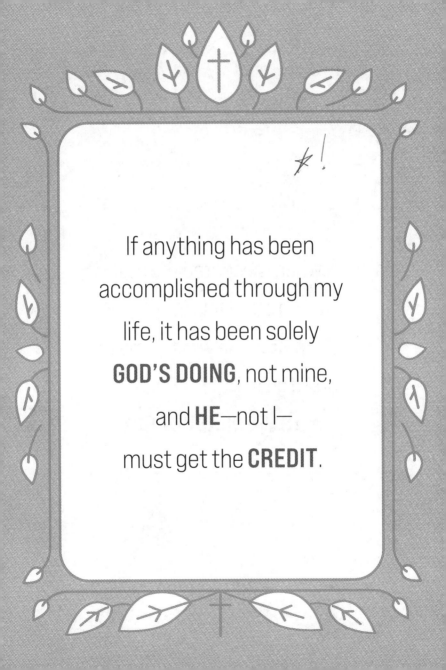

If anything has been accomplished through my life, it has been solely **GOD'S DOING**, not mine, and **HE**—not I— must get the **CREDIT**.

When I accepted the call to ministry, I told God I'd go **ANYWHERE** He wanted me to go. I'd go to **HELL** if He'd give me **SAFE CONDUCT OUT**.

Preaching...involves us in a **SPIRITUAL BATTLE** with the forces of evil. I am always deeply conscious that I am absolutely helpless and that only the **HOLY SPIRIT** can penetrate the minds and hearts of those who are without Christ...All I am doing is **SOWING SEED**. It is God—and only God—who can make that seed bear **FRUIT**.

My calling is to preach the **LOVE** of God and the **FORGIVENESS** of God and the fact that He **DOES FORGIVE** us. That's what the cross is all about, what the resurrection is all about—**THAT'S THE GOSPEL**.

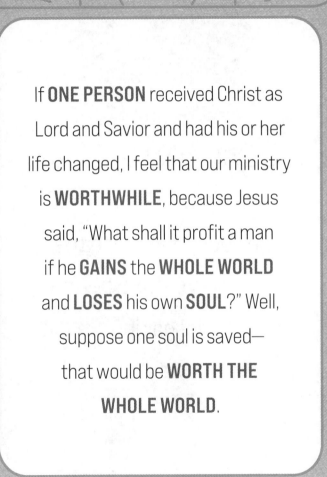

If **ONE PERSON** received Christ as Lord and Savior and had his or her life changed, I feel that our ministry is **WORTHWHILE**, because Jesus said, "What shall it profit a man if he **GAINS** the **WHOLE WORLD** and **LOSES** his own **SOUL**?" Well, suppose one soul is saved— that would be **WORTH THE WHOLE WORLD**.

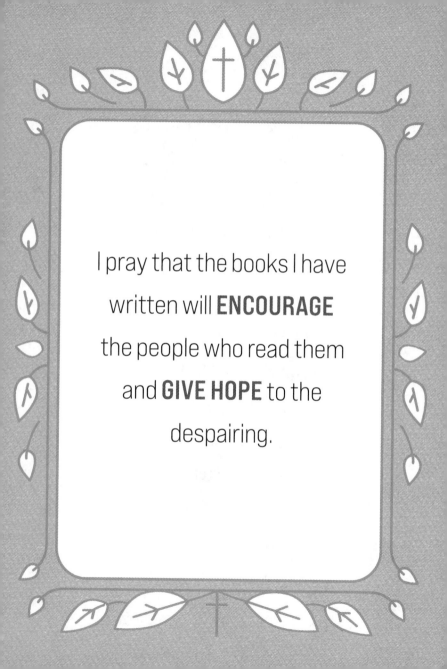

I pray that the books I have written will **ENCOURAGE** the people who read them and **GIVE HOPE** to the despairing.

All of us in Christian ministry need to **LIVE** and **WORK** with **INTEGRITY**. By integrity, I mean the **MORAL VALUE** that makes people the same on the inside as they are on the outside—with no discrepancy between what they **SAY** and what they **DO**, between their **WALK** and their **TALK**. In the Old Testament, Solomon wrote, "The one who lives in integrity lives **SECURELY**, but whoever perverts his ways will be found out" (Proverbs 10:9). "Be sure that your sin will find you out" (Numbers 32:32 NIV). We cannot hide. We think we are hiding from the Lord, but we are not.

God **STILL LOVES** us. He yearns to **FORGIVE** us and **BRING** us back to Himself. He wants to fill our lives with **MEANING** and **PURPOSE** right now. Then He wants us to spend all eternity **WITH HIM** in heaven, **FREE FOREVER** from the pain and sorrow and death of this world.

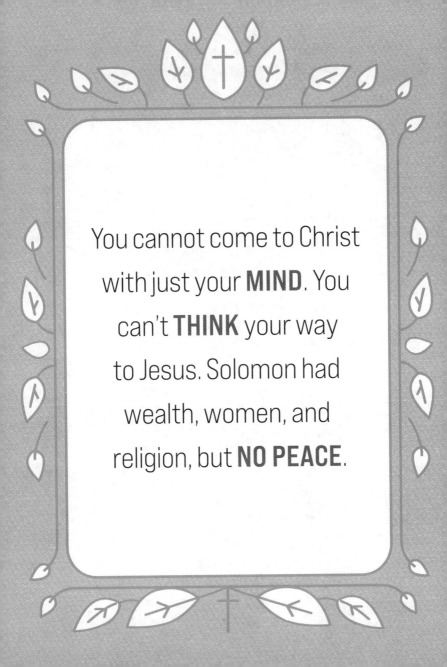

You cannot come to Christ with just your **MIND**. You can't **THINK** your way to Jesus. Solomon had wealth, women, and religion, but **NO PEACE**.

THE STATE OF AMERICA...
AND THE WORLD

The oppressed will not always be forgotten;
the hope of the afflicted will not perish forever.

PSALM 9:18

Much of the world is feeling the effects of terrorism and war right now, but there are other things that are bothering us: disease, poverty, racism, hate, loneliness, AIDS, unemployment, divorce, psychological problems, boredom, murder statistics—the world didn't **STOP SINNING** or getting bored after September 11, 2001. We know that **SOMETHING IS WRONG** with human nature. **SIN** is what's wrong with the world, and only **JESUS CHRIST** can solve it.

In a world of greed, where materialistic values often take first place, pleasure has become a god—and a great premium is placed on cleverness—our **GREATEST NEED** is **MORAL INTEGRITY**. Job said, "Till I die, I **WILL NOT DENY** my integrity" (Job 27:5 NIV). David, the great king of Israel, wrote, "I **WILL WALK** in my integrity" (Psalm 26:11 NKJV).

I believe that if this nation of ours would **TURN TO GOD** in **PRAYER** and in **FAITH**, and would live the Christian life, God would hear from heaven. There is no telling how greatly this nation could **LEAD THE WORLD** if we were living the way God would have us to live.

Christians have often been too **STRIDENT** and **LEGALISTIC**.

I don't think we will have permanent **PEACE** in the world as long as man's heart stays as it is—as long as there is hate and jealousy and greed and lust. You cannot have **PEACE** when man's heart is not at **PEACE**.

As we face a new millennium,
I believe America has gone a long
way down the wrong road. We must
CHANGE ROADS, **TURN AROUND**,
and **GO BACK**. We must **REPENT**
and **COMMIT** our lives to God and
to the moral and spiritual principles
that have made this nation great,
and translate that commitment
into **ACTION** in our homes,
neighborhoods, and our society.

Human nature is the same
the world over, and when
the gospel of Christ is
preached in **SIMPLICITY**
and **POWER**, there is a
RESPONSE in the
human soul.

The deepest problems of the human race are **SPIRITUAL**. They are rooted in man's refusal to seek God's way for his life. The problem is the **HUMAN HEART**, which **GOD ALONE** can change.

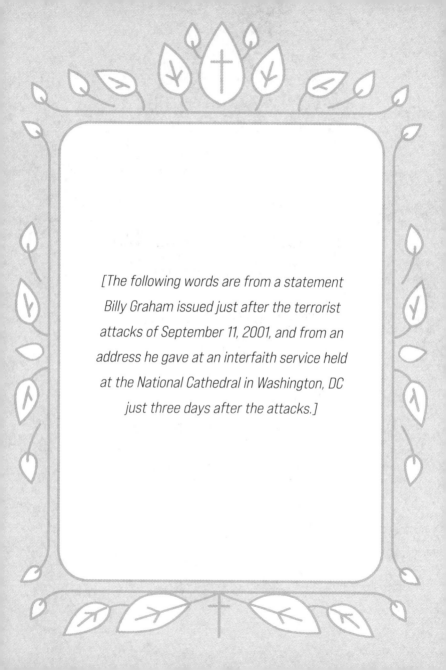

[The following words are from a statement Billy Graham issued just after the terrorist attacks of September 11, 2001, and from an address he gave at an interfaith service held at the National Cathedral in Washington, DC just three days after the attacks.]

In times like these, we realize how weak and inadequate we are, and our greatest need is to **TURN** in **REPENTANCE** and **FAITH** to the God of all **MERCY** and the Father of all **COMFORT**. If ever there was a time for us to **TURN TO GOD** and to **PRAY AS A NATION**, it is **NOW**, that this evil will spread no further. It is also a time for us to remember the words of the psalmist: "God is our **REFUGE** and **STRENGTH**, a very present help in trouble" [Psalm 46:1 NKJV].

We come together today to **AFFIRM** our conviction that God **CARES** about us, whatever our ethnic, religious, or political background may be. The Bible says that He is the "God of **ALL COMFORT**, who comforts us in all our troubles" (2 Corinthian 1:3-4 NIV).

But today, we especially come together in this service to **CONFESS** our need of God. We've **ALWAYS NEEDED** God from the beginning of this nation, but today we need Him especially. We're facing a new kind of enemy. We're involved in a new kind of warfare, and we **NEED THE HELP** of the Spirit of God. The Bible's words are our **HOPE**: "God is our **REFUGE** and **STRENGTH**, a very present **HELP** in trouble. Therefore we will not fear, even though the earth be removed, and though the mountains be carried into the midst of the sea" (Psalm 46:1-2 NKJV).

But how do we understand something like this? Why does God allow evil like this to take place? Perhaps that is what you are asking now. You may even be angry at God. I want to assure you that God **UNDERSTANDS** these feelings that you may have...**GOD CAN BE TRUSTED**, even when life seems darkest. But what are some of the **LESSONS** we can learn?

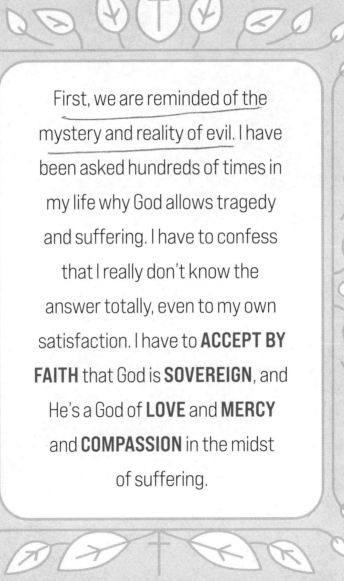

First, we are reminded of the mystery and reality of evil. I have been asked hundreds of times in my life why God allows tragedy and suffering. I have to confess that I really don't know the answer totally, even to my own satisfaction. I have to **ACCEPT BY FAITH** that God is **SOVEREIGN**, and He's a God of **LOVE** and **MERCY** and **COMPASSION** in the midst of suffering.

The lesson about this event is not only about the mystery of iniquity and evil, but secondly, it's a lesson about our **NEED** for **EACH OTHER**. What an example New York and Washington have been to the world these past few days! None of us will ever forget the pictures of our courageous firefighters and police, many of whom have lost friends and colleagues, or the hundreds of people attending or standing patiently in line to donate blood. A tragedy like this could have torn our country apart, but instead it has **UNITED** us, and we've become a **FAMILY**...We are **MORE UNITED** than **EVER BEFORE**.

Finally, difficult as it may be for us to see right now—this event can give a **MESSAGE OF HOPE**—hope for the **PRESENT**, and hope for the **FUTURE**.

Yes, **THERE IS HOPE**. There is hope for the present because I believe the stage has already been set for a **NEW SPIRIT** in our nation. One of the things we desperately need is a **SPIRITUAL RENEWAL** in this country…And God has told us in His Word, time after time, that we are to **REPENT** of our sins and we're to **TURN** to Him, and He will **BLESS** us in a **NEW WAY**.

But there is also a **HOPE** for the **FUTURE**, because of God's **PROMISES**. As a Christian, I have hope, not just for this life, but for **HEAVEN** and the **LIFE TO COME**. And many of those people who died this past week are in heaven right now, and they wouldn't want to come back. It's so **GLORIOUS** and **WONDERFUL**. And that's the hope for all of us who put our **FAITH** in God. I pray that you will have this hope in your heart.

This event reminds us of the brevity and uncertainty of life. We never know when we, too, will be called into eternity...And that's why each of us needs to face our own **SPIRITUAL NEED** and **COMMIT** ourselves to **GOD** and **HIS WILL** now.

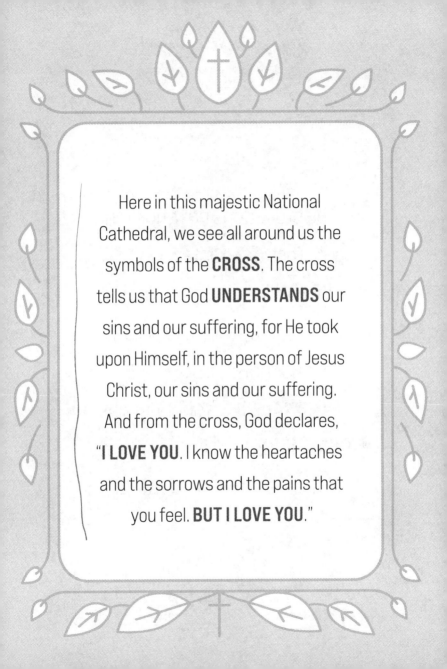

Here in this majestic National Cathedral, we see all around us the symbols of the **CROSS**. The cross tells us that God **UNDERSTANDS** our sins and our suffering, for He took upon Himself, in the person of Jesus Christ, our sins and our suffering. And from the cross, God declares, "**I LOVE YOU**. I know the heartaches and the sorrows and the pains that you feel. **BUT I LOVE YOU**."

The story does not end with the cross, for Easter points us **BEYOND** the tragedy of the cross to the empty tomb. It tells us that there is **HOPE** for **ETERNAL LIFE**, for Christ has **CONQUERED** evil and death and hell. Yes, **THERE IS HOPE**.

I've become an old man now, and I've preached all over the world, and the older I get, the more I **CLING** to that **HOPE** that I started with many years ago and proclaimed in many languages to many parts of the world.

This has been a terrible week with many tears, but also a week of **GREAT FAITH**. My prayer today is that we will feel the **LOVING ARMS** of God wrapped around us, and will know in our hearts that He will **NEVER FORSAKE** us as we **TRUST** in Him.

May God **BLESS** you all.

(Speaking in South Africa)

CHRISTIANITY is not a white man's religion, and don't let anybody ever tell you that it's white or black. **CHRIST BELONGS** to **ALL PEOPLE**!

As long as there is one man in the world who hates another man because of the color of his skin or the shape of his nose or for some other reason, you have the possibility of war. As long as you have men in the world greedy for power, there is potential conflict. I believe that the **GOSPEL OF CHRIST** is the **ONLY POWER** in the world that can **TRANSFORM** the heart of man and make it **LOVE** instead of hate. But will the whole world come to Christ? The Bible teaches otherwise, in my opinion.

We all live under **GRACE** and do the best we can.

PERSONAL REVELATIONS

So I take pleasure in weakness,
insults, catastrophes,
persecutions, and in pressures, because of Christ.
For when I am weak, then I am strong.

2 CORINTHIANS 12:10

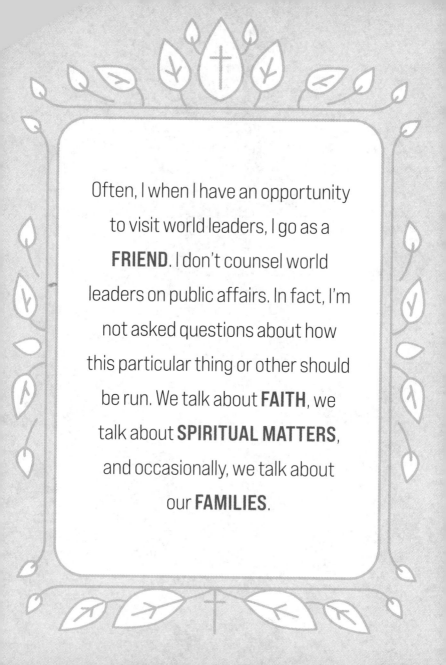

Often, I when I have an opportunity to visit world leaders, I go as a **FRIEND**. I don't counsel world leaders on public affairs. In fact, I'm not asked questions about how this particular thing or other should be run. We talk about **FAITH**, we talk about **SPIRITUAL MATTERS**, and occasionally, we talk about our **FAMILIES**.

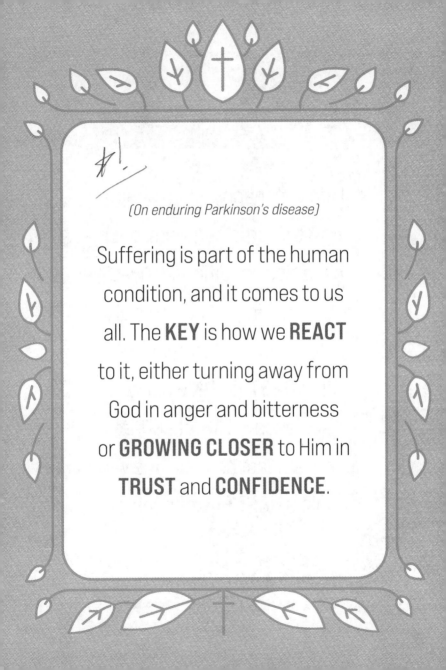

(On enduring Parkinson's disease)

Suffering is part of the human condition, and it comes to us all. The **KEY** is how we **REACT** to it, either turning away from God in anger and bitterness or **GROWING CLOSER** to Him in **TRUST** and **CONFIDENCE**.

I am very happy when people come in large numbers, but I have also conditioned myself to preaching to many empty seats. God often does His **GREATEST WORK** when the audience is **SMALL.** Christ spent at least half his time with just a **HANDFUL** of people.

If I convert any, they won't be real conversions. The **LORD** has to do the **CONVERTING**. The records of the true converts, I believe, are kept in **HEAVEN**. No one will know the answer... until we stand before God on the judgment day.

I am thankful for the **PEACE** of God in my heart, and that could happen to everybody. Whatever your problem, whatever your need, **JESUS** can come into your heart and **FORGIVE** you and **GUARANTEE** you **LIFE**—in this life and also life **BEYOND** this life.

When it comes to the gospel, be **FAITHFUL**, and the **HOLY SPIRIT** will do the **COMMUNICATING** in a way you could never do.

[On popularity and success]

That's one of the first things I'm going to ask God when I get to heaven, because I don't know. I'm the most ordinary person in the world. I'm amazed at it all. To me, **IT'S JUST GOD**. It's the **SOVEREIGNTY** of God in choosing me as He did Jeremiah or Isaiah.

I believe **EVERY WORD** of the Bible from Genesis to Revelation. But the Bible isn't a scientific document; it's written for the **COMMON PEOPLE** in language they can **UNDERSTAND**.

These men did evangelists' work—men like John Wesley, Dwight L. Moody, and William Wilberforce. We've forgotten today how the **EVANGELIST** is as **IMPORTANT** as the **PASTOR** and the **TEACHER**. Of course, I'm not worthy to lick these men's boots…I shouldn't be mentioned.

As I look back over my life, I also have many regrets. I have failed many times, and I would do many things differently. For one thing, I would **SPEAK LESS** and **STUDY MORE**, and I would spend **MORE TIME** with my **FAMILY**. When I look back over the schedule I kept thirty or forty years ago, I am staggered by all the things we did and the engagements we kept.

I thought when I started…
that we could turn the world
UPSIDE DOWN, that the whole
world would turn to God. I am
not quite that naive now. Sin is
a little blacker than I thought it
was, and I am no longer taken
in by statistics. They don't
tell the **STORY**.

I must admit I feel very inadequate at times when talking about **GOD'S DISCIPLINE** through pain…
When those I love have suffered, I have wished I could take their pain as **MY OWN**.

(Did Billy Graham want to preach all his life?)

I asked myself that question for the umpteenth time [many years ago] on one of my nighttime walks around the golf course. I got down on my knees. Then I prostrated myself on the dewy turf. "O God," I sobbed, "if You want me to serve You, **I WILL**." The moonlight, the moss, the breeze, the green, the golf course—all the surroundings stayed the same. No sign in the heavens. No voice from above. But **IN MY SPIRIT** I knew I had been called to the **MINISTRY**. And I knew my answer was **YES**.

I'm not a great man.

I just have a

GREAT MESSAGE.

God knows my **MOTIVE**, and He knows my **HEART**, God uses even a simple presentation that might have been poorly done, and He **APPLIES** it to the human heart.

I know my time on earth will not be over until He calls me home. I admit I don't like the burdens of old age—the slow decline in energy, the physical annoyances, the pain of losing loved ones, the sadness of seeing friends decline. But old age can be a **SPECIAL TIME** of life, and God has **LESSONS** to **TEACH** us through it...I may not be able to do everything I once did (nor does God expect me to), but I am called to be **FAITHFUL** to what I can do.

Many a time under my own preaching I've **RECOMMITTED** my life to the Lord, standing there—because we all have moments when we feel that God is speaking in a very **SPECIAL WAY** to us...and many times I come forward with the people, in my heart, to make a **RECOMMITMENT** in my own life.

God called me to **PREACH**, and I do not intend to do anything else as long as I live.

All that I have been able to do, I owe to **JESUS CHRIST**. I feel I am a **SPECTATOR** watching what **GOD IS DOING**.

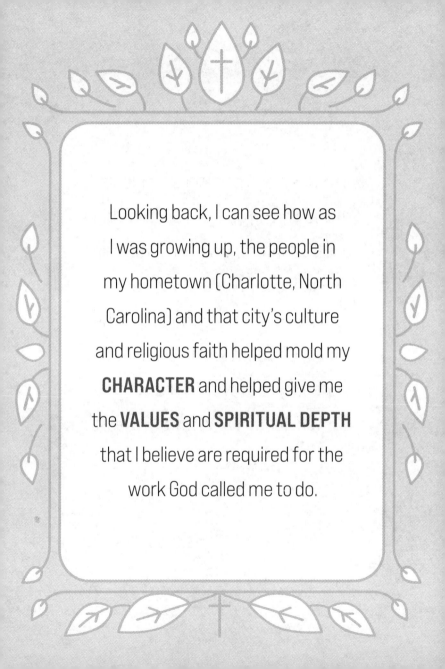

Looking back, I can see how as I was growing up, the people in my hometown (Charlotte, North Carolina) and that city's culture and religious faith helped mold my **CHARACTER** and helped give me the **VALUES** and **SPIRITUAL DEPTH** that I believe are required for the work God called me to do.

I remember a particular incident at the beginning of my ministry. During a 1949 conference in the mountains east of Los Angeles, I had serious doubts about God, Christ, and the Bible. I decided I had to clarify them one way or the other. I had to find **PEACE** about it all in my own heart...

...In the moonlight, I went into the woods. I opened the Bible and laid it on a tree stump. Then I knelt down and said, "O God, I don't understand all that is in this book. Many things seem to be contradictory. I cannot intellectually accept it, but I am going to **ACCEPT** it by **FAITH** as Your Word, Your **INSPIRED, DIVINE WORD**." And I did accept it by faith, and I have never had a doubt since then.

[On books that have influenced him.]

First, I would have to say the **BIBLE**. My wife and I read from the Psalms every day—five psalms and one chapter of Proverbs. The **PSALMS** teach you how to get along with **GOD**; **PROVERBS** teaches you how to get along with **PEOPLE**. I also try to read books on current trends and economics. And every day I read a lot of newspapers and news magazines.

LEARNING was an **INSATIABLE** desire with me. I burned to learn. I am a man still in **PROCESS**.

A keen **SENSE OF HUMOR**
helps us overlook the
unbecoming, understand
the unconventional, tolerate
the unpleasant, overcome
the unexpected, and outlast
the unbearable.

GOD'S LOVE has seen me through sickness, discouragement, and frustration. His love has **SUSTAINED** me during times of disappointment and bewilderment.

The Lord has always arranged my life in a way that keeps me **DEPENDENT** on Him. Over and over again, I went to my knees and asked the **SPIRIT OF WISDOM** for guidance and direction. There were times when I was tempted to flee from problems and pressures and my inability to cope with them; but somehow, even in moments of confusion and indecision, it seemed I could trace the steady hand of **GOD'S SOVEREIGNTY** leading me on.

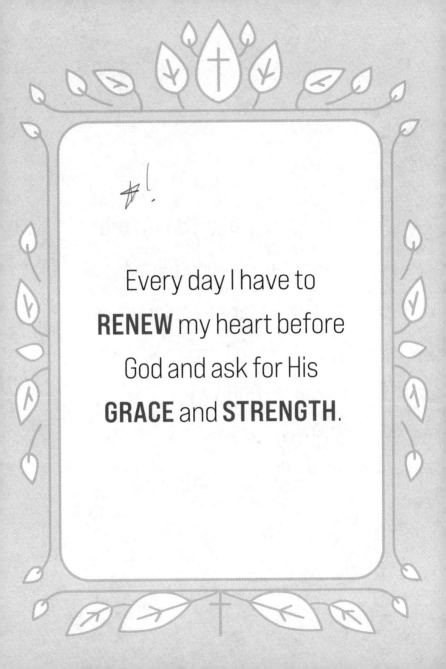

Every day I have to
RENEW my heart before
God and ask for His
GRACE and **STRENGTH**.

I take time each day in the
morning and evening to
READ passages of Scripture
and ask the Lord to **SPEAK**
to me through them—apart
from any preparations of
sermon material.

I believe there is a
worldwide **HUNGER**
for God.

I want people to call me **BILLY**—not Reverend William F. Graham—so that they will feel that they can come to me with any of their problems or needs.

THE POWER OF PRAYER

The LORD has heard my plea for help;
the LORD accepts my prayer.

PSALM 6:9

Prayer is not just asking. It is **LISTENING** for God's orders.

I have learned, I believe, to "**PRAY WITHOUT CEASING**." I find myself constantly in **PRAYER** and **FELLOWSHIP** with God, even while I am talking to other people or doing other things.

Every time my mother prayed with one of us, and every time my parents prayed for their sons and daughters, they were declaring their dependence on God for the **WISDOM** and **STRENGTH** and **COURAGE** to stay in control of life, no matter what circumstances might bring.

We know we cannot do **EVERYTHING** that needs to be done, but in a world that is never free of turmoil, Christ calls us to do **WHAT WE CAN**.

God wants us to have **COMPASSION** on those who are suffering and do what we can to **HELP**.

wow!
 # !

FAITH, more than fighting, can **CHANGE** the course of events today. United, believing, self-humbling, God-exalting **PRAYER** now can change the course of **HISTORY**.

QUOTABLE QUIPS

He said to me,
"Son of man, stand up on your feet
and I will speak with you."

EZEKIEL 2:1

When wealth is lost, nothing is lost. When health is lost, something is lost. When **CHARACTER** is lost, **EVERYTHING** is lost.

Hot heads and cold
hearts never solved
ANYTHING.

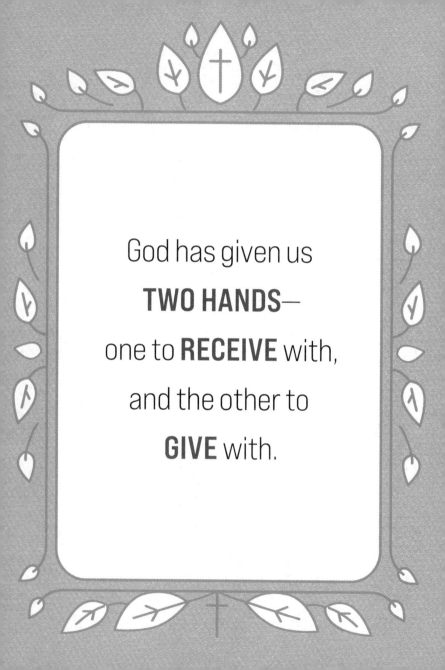

God has given us
TWO HANDS—
one to **RECEIVE** with,
and the other to
GIVE with.

When we come to the
END of ourselves,
we come to the
BEGINNING of God.

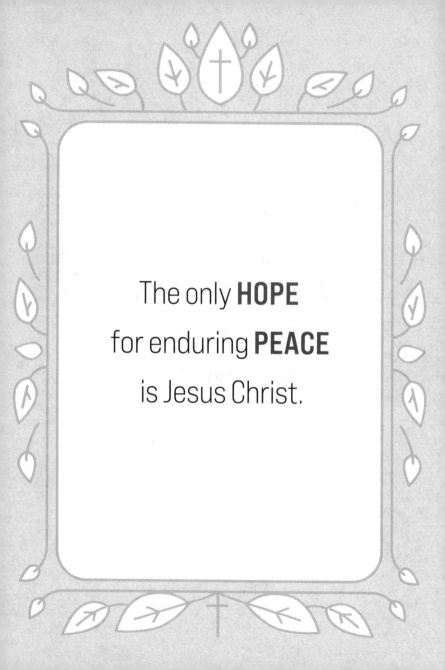

The only **HOPE**

for enduring **PEACE**

is Jesus Christ.

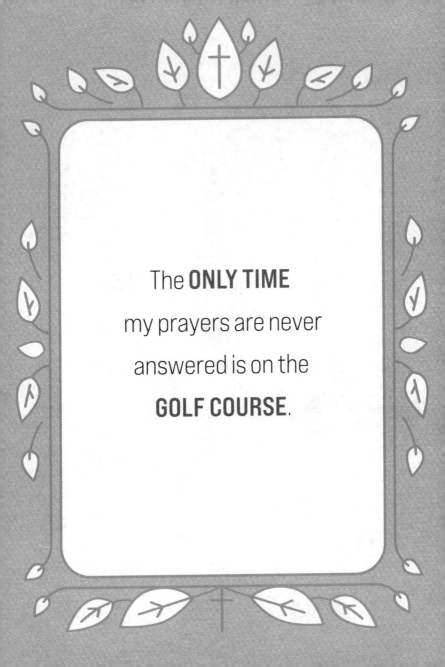

The **ONLY TIME**

my prayers are never

answered is on the

GOLF COURSE.

I am selling the **GREATEST PRODUCT** in the world. Why shouldn't it be **PROMOTED** as well as soap?

There is nothing wrong with
MEN possessing **RICHES**.
The wrong comes when
RICHES possess **MEN**.

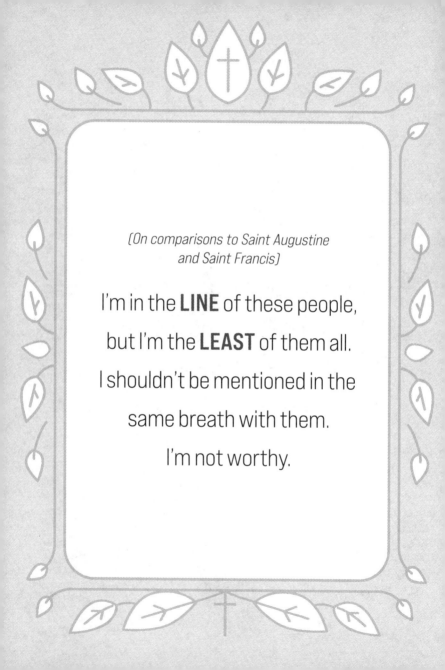

(On comparisons to Saint Augustine and Saint Francis)

I'm in the **LINE** of these people, but I'm the **LEAST** of them all. I shouldn't be mentioned in the same breath with them. I'm not worthy.

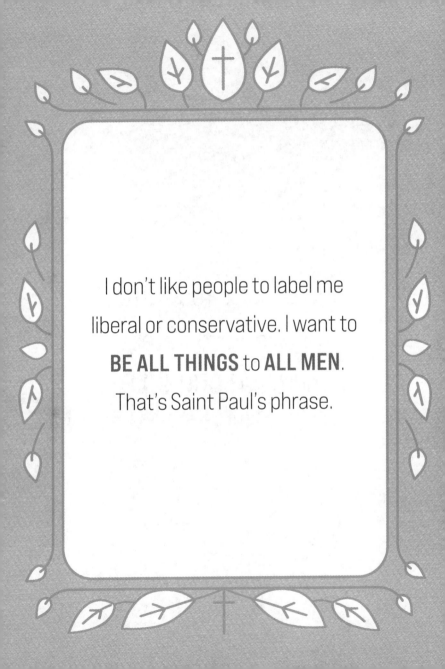

I don't like people to label me liberal or conservative. I want to **BE ALL THINGS** to **ALL MEN**. That's Saint Paul's phrase.

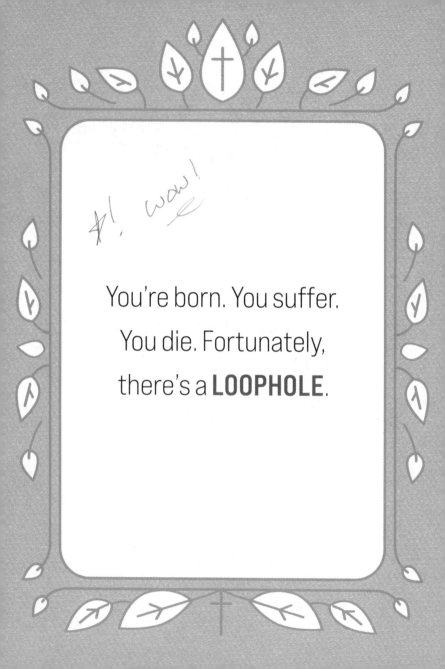

#1, wow!

You're born. You suffer.
You die. Fortunately,
there's a **LOOPHOLE**.

COURAGE is **CONTAGIOUS**.
When a brave man takes
a stand, the spines of
others are stiffened.

MOUNTAINTOPS are for views and inspiration, but fruit is grown in the **VALLEYS**.

CONFRONTING
SOCIAL INJUSTICE

The LORD is a refuge for the oppressed,
a refuge in times of trouble.

PSALM 9:9

Much of my life has been a **PILGRIMAGE**—constantly learning, changing, growing, and maturing. I have come to see in **DEEPER WAYS** some of the implications of my faith and message, not the least of which is the area of human rights and racial and ethnic understanding.

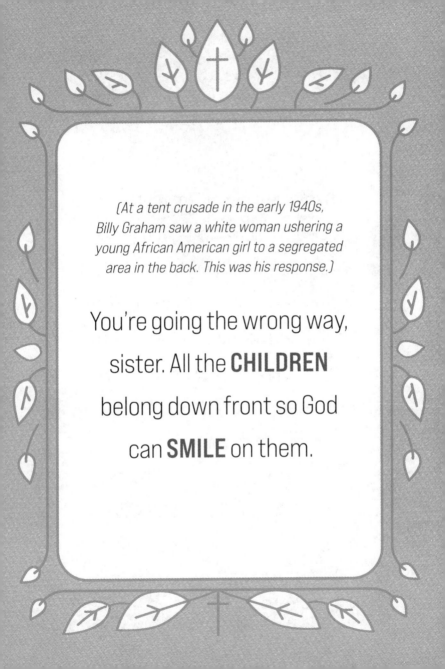

(At a tent crusade in the early 1940s, Billy Graham saw a white woman ushering a young African American girl to a segregated area in the back. This was his response.)

You're going the wrong way, sister. All the **CHILDREN** belong down front so God can **SMILE** on them.

I think it is very evident that Moses had an Ethiopian wife whose skin was dark. I don't think that **CHRIST'S SKIN** was as light as mine or perhaps as dark as the West African's. He was born in a part of the world where his skin was probably more of a brown or swarthy color. To base racial segregation on the Bible, I think, is **RIDICULOUS**...

...Of course you can make the Bible prove anything. You can twist the Scripture all around and take verses and chapters out of context, but the Bible teaches that we are **RIGHTLY** to divide the Word of truth, and that we are to do it with spiritual **DISCERNMENT**. I just cannot find **ANYTHING** to substantiate racial barriers and differences in the Bible.

BIGOTRY of any kind is a **SIN** in God's eyes.

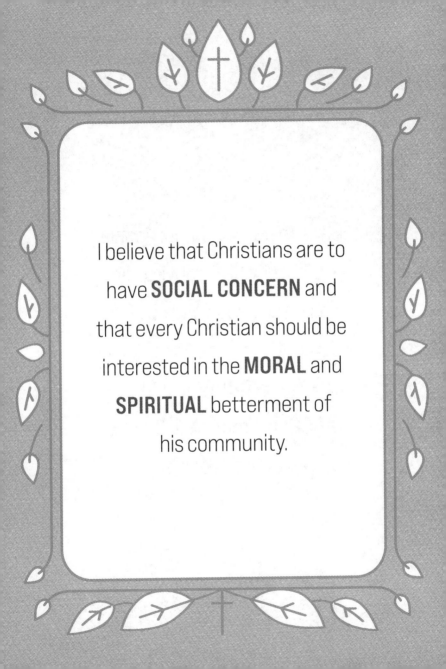

I believe that Christians are to have **SOCIAL CONCERN** and that every Christian should be interested in the **MORAL** and **SPIRITUAL** betterment of his community.

Christ said, "By this all people will know that you are My disciples, if you have **LOVE** for one another" (John 13:15). This affects the **CHURCH**, it affects **RACE**, it affects **ALL SORTS** of areas of life.

There is no scriptural basis for segregation. The ground at the foot of the cross is **LEVEL**, and it touches my heart when I see whites standing **SHOULDER TO SHOULDER** with blacks at the cross.

It has become a byword that the most **SEGREGATED** hour of the week is still **ELEVEN O'CLOCK** Sunday morning.

Racial prejudice, anti-Semitism, or hatred of anyone with different beliefs has **NO PLACE** in the human mind or heart. I urge everyone to **EXAMINE** themselves and **RENEW** their own hearts before God. Only the supernatural **LOVE OF GOD** through changed lives can solve the problems we face in our world.

Hatred and racism are fundamentally **MORAL** and **SPIRITUAL** problems.

FACING THE FUTURE

I have spoken;
yes, I have called him;
I have brought him,
and he will succeed in his mission.

ISAIAH 48:15

The older I get, the more I am asked who will succeed me. Well, the fact is that I am just **ONE** of many **THOUSANDS** who have been called to be evangelists. I don't need a successor, only **WILLING HANDS** to accept the torch I have been carrying.

It is time for the church to use technology to make a statement that in the midst of chaos, emptiness, and despair, there is **HOPE** in the person of **JESUS CHRIST**.

The **MESSAGE** of the gospel never changes—and for good reason: God never changes, and neither does our basic spiritual need, nor His answer to that need. But the **METHODS** of presenting the message do change. In fact, they must change if we are to **KEEP PACE** with a changing world. If we fail to **BRIDGE THE GAP** between us and those we hope to reach, our message will not be communicated, and our efforts will be in vain.

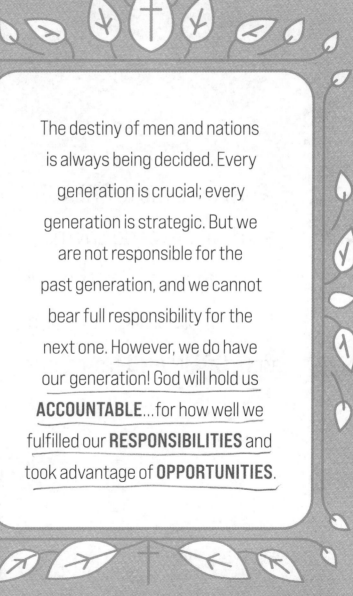

The destiny of men and nations is always being decided. Every generation is crucial; every generation is strategic. But we are not responsible for the past generation, and we cannot bear full responsibility for the next one. However, we do have our generation! God will hold us **ACCOUNTABLE**…for how well we fulfilled our **RESPONSIBILITIES** and took advantage of **OPPORTUNITIES**.

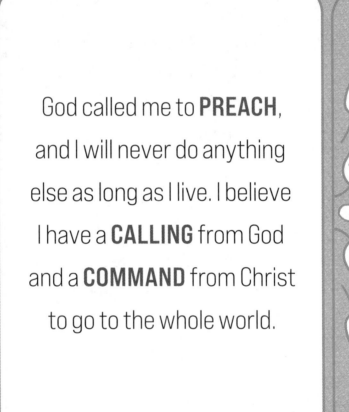

God called me to **PREACH**, and I will never do anything else as long as I live. I believe I have a **CALLING** from God and a **COMMAND** from Christ to go to the whole world.

The more I get older, the closer I get to death, the **HAPPIER** I am. I am filled with **ANTICIPATION**— I'm looking forward to it. One reason is I'll get some **REST**!

What is **HEAVEN** going to be like?
There is a mystery to heaven.
Yet I believe the Bible teaches that
heaven is a **LITERAL PLACE**. Is it one
of the stars? I don't know. I can't even
speculate. The Bible doesn't inform us.
I believe that out there in space, where
there are a hundred billion galaxies,
each a hundred thousand light-years
or more in diameter...

...God can find some place to put us in heaven. I'm not worried about where it is. I know it is going to be where **JESUS** is. Christians don't have to go around discouraged...with their shoulders bent. Think of it—the **JOY**, the **PEACE**, the sense of **FORGIVENESS** that He gives you, and then heaven too.

I might step aside from the organization because it gets beyond me sometimes, but I won't retire from **PREACHING**. We have a lot of little churches around my home in the mountains of North Carolina. They will take me, and I can go there and preach until the day the Lord calls me to heaven. I was **CALLED BY GOD** to do this, and I don't read in the Bible where any of His servants retired.

I look forward to **HEAVEN**... I also look forward to **SERVING GOD** in ways we can't begin to imagine, for the Bible makes it clear that heaven is not a place of idleness. And most of all, I look forward to **SEEING CHRIST** and bowing before Him in praise and gratitude for all He has done for us.

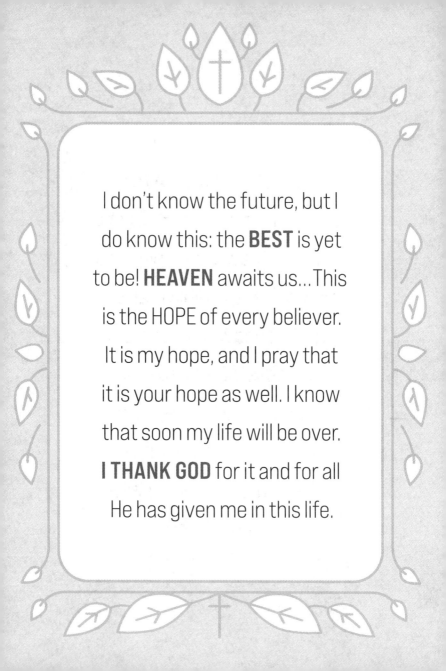

I don't know the future, but I do know this: the **BEST** is yet to be! **HEAVEN** awaits us...This is the HOPE of every believer. It is my hope, and I pray that it is your hope as well. I know that soon my life will be over. **I THANK GOD** for it and for all He has given me in this life.

I'm glad that at the end of it all, the Bible says that Jesus is **COMING BACK** to this earth, and someday He is going to **REIGN**, and there'll be no tears, no suffering, no death...a wonderful future. And I hope I'll meet all of you there. Bring your camera because I may have one too!

I've read the **LAST PAGE** of the Bible. It's all going to turn out **ALL RIGHT**.